BALLADS

OF GOOD DEEDS,

AND OTHER VERSES.

BY

HENRY ABBEY.

NEW YORK:
D. APPLETON & COMPANY,
549 & 551 BROADWAY.
1872.

TO

GEORGE WILLIAM CURTIS

IS DEDICATED

WHATEVER OF GOOD MAY BE IN THESE PAGES.

Old events have modern meanings; only that survives
Of past history which finds kindred in all hearts and lives.

LOWELL.

The instances I produce, how fabulous soever, provided they are possible, serve as well as the true; whether it has really happened or no, at Rome or at Paris, 'tis still within the verge of possibility, and human capacity, which serves me to good use, and supplies me with variety in the things I write.

MONTAIGNE.

CONTENTS.

The author thinks it no more than just to give, with the titles of the pieces, the names of the publications in which they first appeared.

THE ROMAN SENTINEL.

DEATH or dishonor, which is best to taste?
A Roman sentinel in Pompeii,
When God's hot anger laid that city waste,
Answered the question, and resolved to die.
His duty was, upon his post to bide
Till the relief came, let what might betide.

He stood forgotten by the fleeing guard,
Choosing that part which is the bitterest still,
His face with its fixed purpose cold and hard,
Cut in the resolute granite of his will.

"Better," he said, "to die, than live in shame;
Death wreathes fresh flowers round a brave man's
name."

Life is the wave's deep whisper on the shore,
Of a great sea beyond. The sentry saw
That day the light in broad sails hoisted o'er
The drifting boat of dawn; nor dreamed the flaw,
The puff called death, would blow him with them by
Out to the boundless sea beyond the sky.

The sentry watched the mountain's fire-gashed
cheeks,
And saw come up the sand's entombing shower.
The storm darts out its red tongue when it speaks,
And fierce Vesuvius, in that wild hour,

Put forth its tongue of flame, and spoke the word
Of hatred to the city from the Lord.

The gloom of seventeen centuries skulked away,
  And standing in a marble niche was found
A skeleton in armor all decay;
  The soulless skull was by a helmet crowned,
Cleaving thereon with mingled rust and sand,
And a long spear was in the crumbling hand.

In Pompeii are beasts of stone with wings,
  Paved streets with marble temples on each side,
Baths, houses, paintings, monuments of kings;
  But the arched gate whereat the sentry died,
The rusted spear, and helmet with no crest,
Are better far to see than all the rest.

O heart, whatever lot to thee God gives,
  Be strong, and swerve not from a blameless way;
Dishonor hurts the soul that ever lives,
  Death hurts the body that is kin with clay.
Though Duty's face is stern, her path is best:
They sweetly sleep who die upon her breast.

THE FRENCH MARSHAL.

McMAHON up the street of Paris came,
In triumph from Magenta. Every one
Had heard and praised the fearless marshal's name,
And gloried in the deeds that he had done.
Crowds packed the walks, and at each separate glass
A face was set to see the hero pass.

Grand music lifted in the morning air
Its eloquent voice. Loud-mouthed bells were rung,
Guns boomed till echoes welcomed everywhere;
On buildings and in streets proud flags were hung,

Half like the flags of brain-silk wrought with gold,
That hang on Shakespeare's pages, fold on fold.

But while the marshal up the street made way,
  There came a little girl clothed all in white,
Bringing in happy hands a large bouquet;
  Her flower-sweet face seemed fragrant with de-
      light.
Well pleased, the soldier, dark and fierce at need,
Raised up the child before him on his steed.

The pearly necklace of her loving arms
  She bound on him, and laid her Spring-like head
Against the Autumn of his cheek, with charms
  Of smile and mien; while to his shoulder fled
Her gold loose hair with flowers like jewels set,
And made thereon a wondrous epaulet.

He seemed more like an angel than a man,
  As, father-like, he paid back each caress;
Better than all his deeds in war's red van,
  Appeared this simple act of tenderness.
The people cried "Huzza!" and did not pause
Until the town seemed shaken with applause.

So, from this hour, the general became
  The boast of the enthusiastic crowd;
Each gave some flower of praise to deck his fame;
  They knew him brave—though often cold and proud;
But looked not for the kindness undefiled
That he had beamed upon the loving child.

O cynic, deem no more the world all base,
  And scoff no more with either tongue or pen;

You do not see the face behind the face.
  If God exists, there must be noble men;
And many, who to us seem hard and cold,
Have sunshine in their hearts as pure as gold.

THE DRAWBRIDGE-KEEPER.

DRECKER, a drawbridge-keeper, opened wide
The dangerous gate to let the vessel through;
His little son was standing by his side,
Above Passaic River, deep and blue,
While in the distance, like a moan of pain,
Was heard the whistle of the coming train.

At once brave Drecker worked to swing it back,
The gate-like bridge that seems a gate of death;
Nearer and nearer, on the slender track,
Came the swift engine, puffing its white breath.

Then, with a shriek, the loving father saw
His darling boy fall headlong from the draw.

Either at once down in the stream to spring
  And save his son, and let the living freight
Rush on to death, or to his work to cling,
  And leave his boy unhelped to meet his fate—
Which should he do? Were you as he was tried,
Would not your love outweigh all else beside?

And yet the child to him was full as dear
  As yours may be to you—the light of eyes,
A presence like a brighter atmosphere,
  The household star that shone in love's mild skies—
Yet, side by side with duty stern and grim,
Even his child became as naught to him.

For Drecker, being great of soul and true,
Held to his work, and did not aid his boy,
Who, in the deep, dark water, sank from view.
Then from the father's life went forth all joy;
But, as he fell back pallid with his pain,
Across the bridge in safety passed the train.

And yet the man was poor, and in his breast
Flowed no ancestral blood of king or lord;
True greatness needs no title and no crest
To win from men just honor and reward;
Nobility is not of rank, but mind,
And is inborn and common in our kind.

He is most noble whose humanity
Is least corrupted. To be just and good

The birthright of the lowest born may be.
  Say what we can, we are one brotherhood,
And, rich or poor, or famous or unknown,
True hearts are noble, and true hearts alone.

THE GALLEY-SLAVE.

THERE lived in France, in days not long now
dead,
A farmer's sons, twin-brothers, like in face;
And one was taken in the other's stead
For a small theft, and sentenced in disgrace
To serve for years, a hated galley-slave—
Yet said no word his prized good name to save.

Trusting remoter days would be more blessed,
He set his will to wear the verdict out,
And knew most men are prisoners at best,
Who some strong habit ever drag about

Like chain and ball; then meekly prayed that he
Rather the prisoner he was should be.

But best resolves are of such feeble thread,
  They may be broken in Temptation's hands.
After long toil, the guiltless prisoner said:
  "Why should I thus, and feel life's precious
      sands
The narrow of my glass, the present, run,
For a poor crime that I have never done?"

Such questions are like cups, and hold reply;
  For when the chance swung wide the prisoner
      fled,
And gained the country road, and hastened by
  Brown furrowed fields and skipping brooklets
      fed

By shepherd clouds, and felt 'neath sapful trees
The soft hand of the mesmerizing breeze.

Then, all that long day having eaten naught,
  He at a cottage stopped, and of the wife
A brimming bowl of fragrant milk besought.
  She gave it him; but, as he quaffed the life,
Down her kind face he saw a single tear
Pursue its wet and sorrowful career.

Within the cot he now beheld a man
  And maiden also weeping. "Speak," said he,
"And tell me of your grief; for, if I can,
  I will disroot the sad, tear-fruited tree."
The cotter answered: "In default of rent,
We shall to-morrow from this roof be sent."

Then said the galley-slave: "Whoso returns
  A prisoner escaped, may feel the spur
To a right action, and deserves and earns
  Proffered reward. I am a prisoner!
Bind these my arms, and drive me back my way,
That your reward the price of home may pay."

Against his wish the cotter gave consent,
  And at the prison-gate received his fee;
Though some made it a thing for wonderment
  That one so sickly and infirm as he,
When stronger would have dared not to attack,
Could capture this bold youth and bring him back.

Straightway the cotter to the mayor hied,
  And told him all the story, and that lord
Was much affected, dropping gold beside
  The pursed, sufficient silver of reward;

Then wrote his better in authority,
Asking to set the noble prisoner free.

'Tis said our galley-slave was soon released,
  And wedded her with love, the good and fair,
The cotter's daughter, when his store increased.
  The brother-twin, shamed one for him should bear
A dungeon's gloom, had turned to doing well,
And no more shadows on these households fell.

There is no nobler, better life on earth
  Than that of conscious, meek self-sacrifice.
Such life our Saviour, in His lowly birth
  And holy work, made His sublime disguise,
Teaching this truth, still rarely understood:
'Tis sweet to suffer for another's good.

THE STOWAWAY BOY.

WHEN three days forth upon the salty sea,
There came out to the deck a little boy;
Not wherewithal to pay his way had he,
Yet looked up to the broad free sky with joy.
His face was bright and fair, for what is good
Shines out and fears not to be understood.

But on the boy a doubting eye was cast,
And soon there questioned him the master's mate:
He said that his step-father, near a mast
Had hidden him, with food, and bade him wait

Within the place until they reached the shore,
Where a kind aunt would give him from her
store.

The mate was slow to feel the story true,
And thought the sailors gave the boy his food,
And often questioned him before the crew;
The boy replied with steadfast fortitude.
At last the mate avowed the glaring lie
Should be confessed or else the boy must die.

Thereat he bade a sailor fetch a rope,
And, pointing to the yard-arm, sternly said:
"Boy, in ten minutes you will be past hope,
And know the solemn silence of the dead,
Unless you speak, and spurn the lie away."
The boy knelt down and asked if he might pray.

Above its hell of fire the tortured steam
  Shrieked, hissed, and groaned in terror and in pain;
Yet worked the ship's great muscles, shaft and beam.
  The vessel seemed a sea-gull or a crane
Beating the denser air that floods the world,
And round and round her watery wings were whirled.

The sky bent over the contented sea,
  And, like the boy's face, was both pure and clear;
The ship's folk gathered round him anxiously,
  The Lord's Prayer from his earnest lips to hear.
The mate, in tears, by trouble sore oppressed,
Caught up the boy and clasped him to his breast!

Truth's simple grandeur is her priceless wear,
And virtue is the crown upon her head;
So plain is she that even a child may dare
To take her hand and go where she will tread.
Not her shall serpent Error fascinate,
She strikes it down and rules in Time and Fate.

Cling thou to Truth and keep her rigid line,
Nor pander to the false on either side;
Truth dwells with Wisdom, makes the face to shine,
Leads on to honor, is to God allied;
Oh, in thy trial hour, whate'er befall,
Trust her with firm faith, and all in all.

THE EMIR'S CHARITY.

IN Samarcand, the nether Morning Star,
There lived a vizier, treasurer of the king,
Who did not wed until the treasurer, Time,
Had counted down to him his fortieth year.
His loving bride was younger by a score
Of such good coin, and beautiful as dawn.
Mismatched the twain, for she was generous,
And sent no beggar empty from the house;
Yet gave her own, nor touched her husband's
gold.
But he, the treasurer, was miserly,

And tightened up the purse-strings as he said:
"I too must beg unless you cease to give."

The emir in disguise once passed that way,
And, hearing of the kindness of the wife,
Had will to test it. Knocking at the door,
No wife appeared; but in her stead, in wrath,
The vizier, cursing the rag-clad, crust-fed churl
Who dared to seek for dole and break his peace;
Then stroked his beard, and swore by Tamerlane,
By the silk cerements and the sacred tomb,
That Charity herself should cease to be.

"Hold!" quoth the beggar; "say not so of her.
I pray rather that upon the street,
Yea, on the crowded corners of the street,
She yet will stand, this virgin, Charity,

And, hearing her true words, the people there
Will all espouse her cause, and make the world
Mount up and spurn the level of to-day.
Despise no man who asks alms at thy door;
A precious diamond may be meanly set.
It does not soil the angels' holy wings
To hover round the poor. I doff disguise!
Behold, I am the emir! yet, to prove
I am not all devoid of charity,
Still keep the boon of office that I gave."

Hearing a stranger's voice, the wife came forth,
And saw her husband kneeling on the step,
And knew the emir's kind and thoughtful eyes,
And smiled on him and kissed his gentle hand.
And from that day, the alms-folk testify,
No string was tightened round the portly purse;

But evermore the wife, with cheering smiles
Doled bountifully to the grateful poor,
Until, at last, when at the door of heaven
She knocked, herself a beggar, Allah smiled
And gave her alms of everlasting peace.

THE KING'S SACRIFICE.

FOR seven years the drought had parched the land,
Yet day by day the sun blazed overhead,
A fire-eyed fiend of fire with flaming brand.
The stretching worm was by toothed famine fed.
No green thing grew, for starved men tilled the mould
In the dry beds where once the rivers rolled.

The fakirs of the swart, abundant gods,
And seers, the consulters of the stars,

In contrite sackcloth, bearing serpent-rods,
Cleft the close air with words like scimitars:
"The gods demand a human sacrifice—
No rain will fall until the victim dies."

The wise king sat in council on his throne,
And heard the false priests going up and down:
"A life!" he cried. "Must ever blood atone?
I hate its clotted stain upon a crown.
Yet, if I hold my peace, and, at their shrine,
A life be offered, all the stain were mine!

"Lo, it is somewhat more to be a king,
Than gleam in robes of office, sit in state,
Be first in pomps, and rule in every thing.
To love the people, that alone is great!

So I, to prove my love, and give you rain,
Proclaim myself the victim to be slain!"

The feigned wrath of their idols to assuage,
  Forth for his death they led their upright king;
Kind Time, the snail to youth, the bird to age,
  Had touched him lightly with its passing wing.
Youthful in age he looked, bright-eyed, smooth-
    browed,
As for the sacrifice he knelt and bowed.

Then, while the headsman held aloft the blade,
  A cloud, wet-laden, stole before the sun,
And on the weapon, with a hand of shade,
  Laid dusky seizure; for the Fates had spun
A longer, royal thread. The cloud amain
Scattered aslant its crystal load of rain.

So fear not thou, rather than stain thy soul,
  To yield the empty vapor of thy breath.
Hither the years, but thither ages roll,
  Beyond the pale-lit stream of useful death.
Better to suffer than to do a wrong;
Fear not, O heart, to suffer and be strong.

THE SINGER'S ALMS.

IN Lyons, in the mart of that French town,
  Years since, a woman leading a fair child,
Craved a small alms of one, who, walking down
  The thoroughfare, caught the child's glance, and
    smiled
To see, behind its eyes, a noble soul.
He paused, but found he had no coin to dole.

His guardian angel warned him not to lose
  This chance of pearl to do another good;
So as he waited, sorry to refuse
  The asked-for penny, there aside he stood,

And with his hat held as by limb the nest,
He covered his kind face, and sang his best.

The sky was blue above, and all the lane
  Of commerce where the singer stood was filled,
And many paused, and, listening, paused again,
  To hear the voice that through and through
    them thrilled.
I think the guardian angel helped along
That cry for pity woven in a song.

The singer stood between the beggars there,
  Before a church, and, overhead, the spire,
A slim perpetual finger in the air
  Held toward heaven, land of the heart's desire,
As though an angel, pointing up, had said,
"Yonder a crown awaits this singer's head."

The hat of its stamped brood was emptied soon
  Into the woman's lap, who drenched with tears
Her kiss upon the hand of help. 'Twas noon,
  And noon in her glad heart drove forth her fears.
The singer pleased, passed on, and softly thought,
"Men will not know by whom this deed was wrought."

But when at night he came upon the stage,
  Cheer after cheer went up from that wide throng,
And flowers rained on him. Naught could assuage
  The tumult of the welcome, save the song
That for the beggars he, with covered face,
Had sung while standing in the market-place.

Oh, cramped and narrow is the man who lives
  Only for self, and pawns his years away

For gold, nor knows the joy a good deed gives;
  But feels his heart shrink slowly, day by day,
And dies at last, his bond of fate outrun;
No high aim sought, no worthy action done.

But brimmed with molten brightness like a star,
  And broad and open as the sea or sky,
The generous heart. Its kind deeds shine afar,
  And glow in gold in God's great book on high.
And he who does what good he can each day,
Makes smooth and green and strews with flowers
    his way.

THE EMPEROR'S MERCY.

WHEN Theodosius, who ruled the land,
Had laid exactions, deemed too hard to bear,
On Antioch, angry revolt was planned,
And, hoarsely surging to the public square,
The folk dashed on the statues of the crown,
The ruler's and his wife's, and broke them down.

But, when the tide of fury ebbed away,
Upon all hearts there lay a stranded dread.
The dwellers sorrowed at their deed that day,
And on Thought's canvas saw their danger spread.

A sombre painter, born of fault, is Fear,
That magnifies the ills it makes appear.

So Bishop Flavianus, strong of pen,
  In truth a poet, but who nobly found
That he a higher good could do to men
  In preaching Christ, than if with laurel crowned,
Left Antioch, and hastened on his way,
The ruler's wrath to soften and allay.

He reached Constantinople, and was led
  Before the emperor, who heard his plea:
"We place a wreath on even the wicked dead.
  Since wrong, repented of, no more can be,
On our dead wrong let now thy pardon rest
Like a white wreath upon a silent breast."

With darkened look the ruler made reply:
  "Pretence cannot make sweet what sooth is sour.
Not till forgiveness comes can injury die;
  And, though of pardon one should place the
      flower
Where, in repentance hearsed, a wrong is lain,
The wrong may rise to violence again.

"You have cast down the statues cut from stone,
  And, of the metal of ingratitude,
Reared a colossal shame. This shall be thrown,
  In turn, prone to the earth, by vengeance rude.
Let no sleek speech blind Justice enervate!
I am resolved. My word is law and fate."

With saddened soul the bishop turned away;
  But, knowing that, of boys with harps, a choir

Before the emperor made glad the day,
  While he reclined at meat, there came desire,
Through these, the singers, to renew his plea,
And with a song the threatened city free.

Straightway, with loving care, he wrote an ode,
  Glad that, at last, to turn the wheel of use,
The sparkling brook of his clear numbers flowed.
  "That art is best," he said, "which can induce
To serviceable ends. Of old, art's kings
Were fain to do good work on useful things."

The rhyme was finished, and the balanced words
  By music voiced, whose plaintive undertone
Was like the twilight notes of woodland birds.
  When from his potent, golden-curtained throne,

The ruler came to feast, like seraphim
The choir with harps took up the song for him.

They sang the wrong and fears of Antioch,
  And of the awe of love repentance brings;
They woke, with fingers swift, a flying flock,
  The fine compassion of the trembling strings.
The ruler cried, "Oh, cease thy bitter song,
For I forgive the city of the wrong!"

Spirit of Mercy, child of love divine,
  By whom, through Christ, the weary may find
      rest,
Oh, make our souls in unison with thine,
  And enter in and dwell in every breast;
And let it need no more the power of art
To rouse thee from thy slumber in the heart.

THE BEDOUIN'S REBUKE.

NEBAR, a Bedouin of noble heart,
That from all men received of praise the fee,
Owned a brave horse, with which he would not part,
Because from death he once had run him free.
The man and beast were friends, and it is vice
To sell our friend or friendship for a price.

The horse was black and strong, his step was proud;
His neck was arched, his ear alert for sound;
His speed the tempest's, and his mane a cloud;
His hoofs woke thunder from the desert ground;

His eyes flashed lightning from their inmost core:
Victor of Distance was the name he bore.

Daher, a Bedouin of another tribe,
  Had often wished to buy this famous beast;
And as he smoked, and heard his friends describe
  Its comely parts and powers, the wish in-
    creased;
But Nebar said the horse should not be sold,
Though offered wealth in camels and in gold.

Then Daher put on rags, and stained his face,
  And went to wait for Nebar, seeming lame.
Him soon he saw approach with daring pace
  Upon the envied horse, and as he came
He cried to him: "For three days on this spot
Have I lain starving—pity me my lot."

And, seeing Nebar stop, said on, "I die—
My strength is gone!" Down Nebar sprang,
And raised him gently, with a pitying sigh,
And set him on his horse. A laugh outrang,
And Daher shouted as he plunged his spurs,
"Fair price refused, one sells at last for burrs."

"Stay! stay!" cried Nebar: Daher paused to hear;
"Since Heaven has willed that you my beast should take,
I wish you joy; but tell no man, for fear
Another who was really starved might make
Appeal in vain; for some, remembering me,
Would fail to do an act of charity."

Oh, sharp as steel to Daher seemed remorse.
He paused a moment, then sprang to the ground,

And with bowed head brought Nebar back his
horse;
And, falling on his honest breast, he wound
His arms about his neck for true amends,
And ever afterward the two were friends.

If all of us, whene'er we suffer wrong,
Should bear it mildly, since God wills it so,
Nor lend our speech to anger, like the song
The morning stars sang life would pass below:
For he who lightly draws the sword of wrath,
Wounds most himself, and crowds with strife his
path.

THE ARTIST'S PRAYER.

WASHINGTON ALLSTON, in a foreign land,
Went to his studio, and knelt to pray,
Starving and weak, with want on either hand.
Conscience had risen in his heart that day,
As unto Saul, when hedged about with foes
The accusing prophet out of death arose.

Within the vast cathedral of the night,
The stars, the altar-lamps, their thanks outshine;
Yet he, the painter, from whose soul shone bright
The nobler fire of genius, God's divine

And greatest gift to man, had never cast
One ray of gratitude for mercies past.

"I have been most ungrateful, Lord," he said,
"And, housed in self, I have forgotten Thee;
Yet now, I pray, vouchsafe me this day's bread,
And I will pay of my poor thanks the fee,
As I now pay for favors heretofore—"
The irreverent knocker clanked upon the door.

Marquis of Stafford there the threshold crossed.
"Who bought," he asked, "your 'Angel Uriel?'"—
"It is not sold."—"Not sold! Then name the cost,
And I shall make it mine." So it befell
That friendship followed, and the painter came
To better days, and had the use of fame.

Oh, half the good that daily blooms for men
  Is from the seed of prayer. God gives success
Often to test our gratitude, and then
  Withdraws it, if we lack, with tenderness;
Yet if we turn, and of His help implore,
A blessing is already at the door.

THE JEW'S FAITH.

IN the old days, in Alexandria, dwelt
    Nicanor, a self-sacrificing Jew,
Who honestly in every matter dealt,
  Until his spreading tree of fortune grew
Beyond the small dwarfed stature of his needs,
And each bent bough bore reproducing seeds.

And then, like him who walking up the way
  Turns round to question him that comes behind,
He, turning, faced his heart and asked one day:
  "What shall I make my duty? Fixed, my mind

Demands its aim must now be understood,
For every man should live for some set good."

Thereto his heart made answer: "Lips are fair;
  Make two vast doors for lips, and go with them,
And hinge them on the Temple's mouth, that
    there
  They long may name thee to Jerusalem:
With lily-work and palm thy doors be made,
And both with beaten copper overlaid."

In time the lips were wrought, and, with much gain,
  He stowed them on a bark, and sailed away;
And saw the land fade forth from off the main,
  While 'neath the sun the rippled waters lay
Like the great roof that Solomon of old
Built on the Temple, spiked with goodly gold.

When certain days flew west a storm came up,
  And night was like a black and fearful cave
Where Powers of Awe held banquet: as cloud-cup
  Struck waved cloud-cup, the clash deep thunder
      gave,
And spilled the wine of rain. The thrilling gloom
Was filled with loud though unseen wings of doom.

Then said the master of the worried keel:
  "Vile Jew, thy doors are heavy: they must go!"
Nicanor cried: "Here, at thy feet, I kneel,
  And crave of thee to spare them. I will throw
My goods away and gold, my proof of thrift;
But spare the doors, to God my humble gift.

"Despise me not; for he who scorns a Jew
  Without just cause, himself shall be despised."

Thereat his gains he gathered up and threw
  Into the sea, till all were sacrificed
Except his gift; but still the Pan-like blast
Piped on the reed of each divested mast.

Up spoke the sailors to their master dark:
  "We late made mention to our gods of this,
And they require we shall unload the bark
  Of the vile Jew and all that may be his."
As the dread judgment meek Nicanor heard,
He radiantly smiled, but said no word.

Then in the deep the lofty doors were thrown.
  Nicanor prayed, "I put my trust in Thee!"
And sprang out to the storm, and scaled alone,
  'Gainst Death, the unceasing rampart of the sea.

He sank and rose; but, going down once more,
His wandering hand seized on a drifting door.

Dripping and weak, he crawled upon his float,
  And heard the cry go past, "The ship is lost!"
Then shrieks, death-ended. Swords of storm that
    smote
  Were now soon sheathed, while flags of foam
    that tossed
Were furled in peace, and good Nicanor found
The lip there kissed the sweet and certain ground.

A cape ran out, a long, rock-sinewed arm
  That buffeted the sea, and this had caught
The Jew and both his doors; and, free of harm,
  He stood in dawn's gray surf. Stout help he
    brought,

And, passing safely inland far and fast,
The gifts were on the Temple hinged at last.

Long centuries succeed, and Herod, king,
  Rose to rebuild the Temple. For rough stone,
He reared stone snow, white marble. Each pure thing
  He beautified. Nicanor's doors alone
Were left. "These," said the wise high-priests,
        "shall be
For a memorial of piety."

Danger ennobles duty simply done,
  And is a test wherein is cast for proof
The ore of faith. There comes no fear to one
  Whose faith is true, for though upon that roof
Where only Christ of flesh has firmly trod,
He stands on rock who puts his trust in God.

THE RINGER'S VENGEANCE.

IN Florence, years ago, there dwelt a youth,
  Broad-shouldered, fair in face, and tall and strong,
Plighted to one he loved in very truth—
  A lady proud, whose black hair, fine and long,
Some said, was like a flag, that waved or fell
Above her heart's deceitful citadel.

To these the days were bright, as days may be
  To all who love as lovers always should;
But one fell night a cry of dread ran free,
  And one beloved in deadly peril stood.

About her house the hot flames roared and broke
In waves of fire that dashed a spray of smoke.

Prone on the seat within her oriel
  The lady sank; then he, her lover, came
And lowered her to the street; but it befell
  That, as he turned back 'mid the leaping flame,
The roof fell in, and to the crackling floor
The heavy beams his sturdy body bore.

They brought him forth, all bleeding, burned, and crushed,
  And long he lay, and neither stirred nor spoke;
Not yet by wayward death his heart was hushed,
  But seemed a blacksmith pounding, stroke by stroke,

And working on through night from sun to sun,
Until his fateful labor would be done.

"My love," soon mused the youth, "must love
me well,
She will be true and kind to me, I know,
And life will brim with sunshine where we dwell;
All's for the best, since God has willed it so.
I long once more to see her sweet and fair,
And kiss the ripples of her mouth and hair.

"Dear love! she will behold me with her heart,
And pity me, because my lot is hard;
She will not look upon this outer part
That for her sake is crippled and is scarred."
False hope, poor heart!—for, when the lady came,
She turned away with loathing, to her shame.

As one in swamps sees fire-flies flare in gloom,
  And fancies them the street-lights of a town
Whose spires and domes among the shadows loom,
  Yet finds at dawn but lowland, so came down
The hope-built future, and the sufferer found
Beneath his feet the waste and useless ground.

Yet Sorrow brings no dagger in her hand
  To slay the heart with whom she comes to
      dwell;
The youth lived on, and he was wont to stand
  Before a church, and listen to the bell
That in a great spire, bright with golden gloss,
Laughed from its yellow throat beneath the cross.

Then loss of wealth with other damage fell,
  And for a beggar's pittance he became

The ringer of the wide-mouthed, thick-lipped bell,
  Whose noisy somersets he made proclaim
Vesper or mass or lovers to be wed,
Or pulled it with large pity for the dead.

And now they bade him ring a joyful peal,
  For she who once had clothed his heart with
      pain,
Before the altar 'neath the bell would kneel,
  And wed another. Then, for good or bane,
There came two spirits out of east and west,
And wrestled fiercely in the Ringer's breast.

All the long night before the wedding-morn
  He in the belfry stayed and worked, dark-browed,
And, as he looked forth when the day was born,
  The better spirit in his heart was cowed.

The nails were drawn, the beams made weak at last,
That once had held the great bell firm and fast.

The Ringer saw the landscape, and to him
It was a cup, and there the red sun stood,
A drop of splendid wine upon the rim,
And clouds arose, clothed on with cloak and
hood,
And, with their stained lips at the crimson brink,
Seemed monstrous genii who had come to drink.

They came in time with followers in a file,
The happy bridegroom and the smiling bride;
They passed the portal and came up the aisle,
And knelt down at the altar, side by side.
The bride looked up beneath her veil of lace,
And saw with fear the Ringer's livid face.

Then sprang he to the rope to ring her knell,
  With all the inclement anger of his soul;
The huge inverted lily of the bell
  Shook in the gust, and, with a last loud toll,
Fell from its place, and, echoing near and wide,
Crushed 'neath its weight the Ringer and the bride.

Revenge is base and bitter at the core,
  And in a noble mind will never grow;
Yet there are times when it is somewhat more,
  And is almost like justice—for we know
That there are wrongs so deep there seems no cure,
Save in dire retribution swift and sure.

Yet meek Forgiveness, in her gentle reign,
  Repays in time in dividends of good.

Who doubts that, had the Ringer borne his pain,
  He had obtained the noblest brotherhood?
For wrongs that are forgiven in our sin
Are doors where loving angels enter in.

AGNES HATOT.

(A. D. 1390.)

WHEN Might made law in days of chivalry,
Hatot and Ringsdale, over claims to land,
Darkened their lives with stormy enmity;
And for their rights agreed this test to stand:
To fight steel-clad till either's blood made wet
The soil disputed—and a time was set.

But Hatot sickened when the day drew near,
And strength lay racked that once had been his boast.

Then Agnes, his fair daughter, for the fear
  That in proud honor he would suffer most,
Set Will to do the battle in his name,
And leave no foothold for the tread of Shame.

She, at the gray, first coming of the day,
  Shook off still sleep, and from her window gazed.
The west was curtained with night's dark delay;
  A cold and waning moon in silence raised
Its bent and wasted finger o'er the vale,
And seemed sad Death who beckoned, wan and
      pale.

But Hope sails past the rugged coasts of Fear;
  For while awakened birds sang round her eaves,
Our Agnes armed herself with knightly gear
  Of rattling hauberk and of jointed greaves;

Withal she put on valor, that to feel,
Does more for victory than battle-steel.

She had a sea of hair, whose odor sweet,
  And golden softness, in a moonless tide
Went rippling toward the white coast of her
      feet;
  But as beneath a cloud the sea may hide,
So in her visored, burnished helmet, there,
Beneath the cloud-like plume, was hid her hair.

Bearing the mighty lance, sharp-spiked and long,
  She at the sill bestrode her restless steed.
Her kneeling soul prayed God to make her strong,
  And prayer is nearest path to every need.
She clattered on the bridge, and on apace,
And met dread Ringsdale at the hour and place.

They clashed in onslaught. Steel to steel replies.
  The champed bit foams. Rider and ridden fight.
Each feels the instinct in his nature rise
  That in forefront of havoc takes delight.
The lightning of the lances flashed and ran
Until, at last, the maid unhorsed the man.

Then, on her steed, she, bright-eyed, flushed, and glad,
  Her helmet lifted in the sylvan air;
And from the iron concealment that it had,
  The noiseless ocean of her languid hair
Broke with dishevelled spray. The cross and heart,
Jewels that latched her vest, she drew apart.

"Lo, it is Agnes, even I!" she said,
"Who with my trusty lance have thrust you down!
For hate of shame the fray I hazarded;
And yet, not me the victory should crown,
But God, the Merciful, who helps the right,
And lent me strength to conquer in the fight."

Oh, he by all should be accounted base,
Who, for a gift that God has given him,
Takes honor to himself. Of him all trace
Forgetfulness should cancel and bedim.
He steals from Heaven, for self-love makes corrupt,
And dwarfs the soul who of her wine has supped.

But he who gives to God the meed of praise
For proof of gratitude within his heart,

May find success attendant on his ways,
  Shall with the future have a lot and part;
For time his name will brighten, though afar,
As twilight brightens and brings near her star.

NATHAN AND MITHRIDANES.

NATHAN, a wise man, who had nursed with care
A tree of trade that bore sufficient coin,
Lived not alone for self, but thought to share
His wealth with others; so at once to join
His thought to action, where the chief roads crossed
He reared a palace, fair and white as frost.

Here, food he laid, and smooth wine made to flow
For all who came from either east or west;
Beggars were not too base for him to know,
And each was served as an invited guest;

And when at last there broke the parting day,
He doled them gifts, and saw them on their way.

From these mere springs, his fame in rivers flowed,
  And proud Mithridanes, not taking heed
That charities for praise of men corrode
  And lose their virtue, thought the same good
    deed
He too might do and win as high renown,
For Nathan's name was better than a crown.

So he too built a palace wide and high,
  And clad it with the banners of his land;
The prosperous towers grasped the golden sky,
  The fragrant fountains tossed on either hand;
And this, and Nathan's palace, seemed to be
Let down from heaven for deeds of charity.

But proud Mithridanes was envious still,
As Nathan's name was held above his own,
And soon he willed to go to him and kill
The generous man, that he, and he alone
Through the broad world might gain the fame he could
For large munificence and doing good.

See how vile Envy may mislead our hearts,
And feed us with unpalatable sin!
Mithridanes for Nathan's door departs,
And, reaching it, with peace is welcomed in;
Even a parrot, up a stairway heard,
Stabs at his envy with its friendly word.

But ere the hospitable roof was won,
He overtook an ancient on the road.

"Tell me how near my journey now is done;
  I go to Nathan and his praised abode."
"I am his servant," said the old man gray,
"I shall ride forward with you on your way."

This man was Nathan, though unknown to him
  Whose deadly purpose slumbered in his breast;
And often in the park, as day waned dim,
  They met thereafter, one with gloom oppressed,
And talked of Honor and her favorite few,
Till from the commerce wealth of friendship grew.

Here on the root-veined soil-flesh of the world,
  The comer told the white-beard that he sought
The murder of his rival—that, fast furled,
  No more the name of Nathan should be
      caught

And banner-like o'er hill and vale be sent
As the most wise and most benevolent.

"I shall see to it you are gratified,"
  Meek Nathan said, "for, at the bud of day,
Your foe will walk these time-ringed trees beside,
  And you may fall on him, and be away
Before his death is bruited; lest in wrath
They should pursue you, flee the mountain-path."

At morn went forth the guest to slay the host,
  And saw the old man walking mid the trees,
The friend he of all others loved the most.
  "Lo, I am Nathan! great Mithridanes;
Here, where the heart is, pierce me to the hilt;
Pause not with fear, but slay me if thou wilt."

Then at his feet the guest fell prone, with tears:
  "My dearest father, I was proud and base;
Forgive me, for remorse in after-years
  Will rack me, when I think upon thy face!
No more my envy makes a foe of thee,
For I behold thy vast humility."

"Arise!" said Nathan. "Though I do forgive,
  I need not, for, in wishing to excel,
You have done nothing wrong. Proud monarchs live
  Who, to be great, have thought it wise and well
To slay whole armies on the field of strife;
But you have only sought my humble life."

The pleasant jewel of good Nathan's face
  Shone with the inborn lustre of his soul,

And, when the other stood up in his place,
  With full forgiveness round his neck he stole
His amicable arms. Thus malice passed,
And peace had triumphed in its stead at last.

Humility is the excess of love
  We have for others—if that be excess
Which He, who for our help, came from above
  And wore our humbler nature, loved to bless;
But Envy is the coward side of Hate,
And all her ways are bleak and desolate.

BELLEROPHON

SIR EDWARD BULWER LYTTON writes of one
Who strove by charms, and with the aid of ghosts,
Of making gold to find the secret out:
Who drew a magic ring about his crucible,
And while they labored fast at alchemy,
He to beat back the adverse ghosts essayed.
At last, within the circle he had drawn,
Was placed a monstrous Foot, so large, his face
Was level with the instep. All in vain
Each puny effort to drive back the Foot.

Oh, hard for him, who, having once let in
Upon the charmèd circle of the good
The first advance of error, strives to oust
The evil, and make fair the round again:
The giant Foot, stock-still, will not retreat.

And I bethink me him, who in the past,
Before Christ's ransom purchased all our sins,
And in a land that did not know of God,
Upon the Plain of Wandering, the Aleian Plain,
Walked silently beneath the silent stars,
And kept the circle of the good intact,
And to his own heart cogitated thus:

"Antea, wife of Prœtus, tempted me.
She, in the palace, where the fountains are,
Met me at twilight as she walked alone,

Clad with uncinctured robe, adorned with gems,
Perfumed with all the spices of the East.
She made her arms a girdle for my neck,
And, lifting both her small, gold-sandalled feet,
Hung her full weight upon me. Her lips' bud
Bloomed to a crimson rose against my own.
My beard touched her white cheek, while in my ear
She told the eager whisper of her love.

"I put arm's-length between our souls, and hissed
Between set teeth a menace 'gainst all sin.
She left me thus, and went to him, her liege,
And with the broken fragments of her speech—
Bits of the jar that could not hold her tears—
She let it fall that I had done her wrong.

"So, in dire wrath, the fierce king called for
me,
And on a tablet writing fatal characters,
He sent me forth with them beyond his realm,
To Lycia, to the king thereof, who met
And entertained me by the Xanthus' tide.
Nine days of feasting passed, and on the tenth
The tablets were unsealed, their purport known—
And their base appetite is gorged to-day.

"But first the Chimæra I slew invincible.
She was in front a lion, and behind
A dragon, and between the two a goat.
Her breath was gleaming fire that uttered forth,
And burned the woodlands where she passed in
wrath.
And her indeed I slew and gave to death.

I fought with Solymi, the Illustrious,
I slew the man-opposing Amazons,
I turned to naught the secret ambuscade,
And won new lustre to my blameless name.

"But what if I had listened to the queen,
And had become the servant of her wish?
I hold, the soul is like a piece of cloth,
Which, being stained, is stained for evermore—
That nothing can erase the stain of sin.

"Suppose, now being dead, I knelt me down
Upon the first gold step of great Jove's throne,
My soul a piece of cloth within my hands,
All smeared and soiled and stained with Antea's
sin,
And said:

"'Great Jove, accept this cloth, I pray;
Thou madest it. The texture is as fine
As the loose woof of clouds, or the worm's silk.
These blots and stains are most like roses strewn.'

"Then would great Jove make answer, scorning me:
'O fool, and blind! to mock the mighty gods;
For on the golden texture of the soul,
Only a noble deed seems like a flower.'

"Well, whoso wills shall always have his way,
And what was right that I had willed to do."

TO RICHARD GRANT WHITE,

ON READING HIS LIFE OF SHAKESPEARE.

I READ your life of Shakespeare late;
  The clock, swift-handed, showed the hour
Of midnight on the numbered plate,
  And yet your words with pleasant power
Held my attent inviolate.

I seemed to be in Stratford town,
  Our Shakespeare's English Nazareth.
I saw the houses thatched and brown,
  The street whose squalor brought it death.
To my own time the past came down.

I saw the Avon wind and glide,
  And Sir Hugh Clopton's bridge across,
With fourteen arches cool and wide,
  Deep-shadowed in the water's gloss,
Like care that spans some pleasure's tide.

And still the present seemed to me
  The age of Queen Elizabeth,
And on the wall of Trinity
  I saw the painted shape of Death,
The rude, though strong, Dance Macabree.

To Shottery I seemed to stray,
  And passed the house where Shakespeare went,
In idle hours of youthful May,
  To wed himself to discontent
And that fair shrew Ann Hathaway.

I saw his lampoon on the gate
  Of proud Sir Thomas Lucy's park,
And knew he thus would irritate,
  More than deer-stealing after dark,
This pompous Stratford potentate.

Boy-husband, scarcely twenty-one,
  Yet with three children round his knees,
It was full time that he had won
  From Fortune's wheel the bread for these,
For mouths must eat, and work be done.

And by the magic of your book,
  Which was like something seen, not read,
I saw our Shakespeare as he took
  The road for London from the stead,
And his want-shadowed cot forsook.

And by the Aladdin's lamp he bore,
  I saw his wondrous works arise,
Vast palaces of precious store,
  Perfumed with flowers, adorned with dyes
Of thoughts that are for evermore.

At Globe or Blackfriars, in his play
  Of "As You Like It," him the part
Of faithful *Adam*, sear and gray,
  I saw impersonate, with art
That showed a nature sweet as May.

I saw him when he meekly wrote
  With Greene and Marlowe and the rest.
Of his own power he took no note;
  For wounded pride within his breast
He sought a simple antidote—

And that to dwell in Stratford town,
  And live at ease, a gentleman,
By poverty no more held down,
  No more in dread beneath the ban
Of vain Sir Lucy's stony frown.

And so through life the poet passed,
  To win a goal of poor pretence;
Like that old sculptor, who once cast,
  For low and paltry recompense,
A statue deemed divine at last.

RECOMPENSE.

IN spring, two robins from the warmer lands
  Builded a nest upon an unsafe limb
Of the tall tree that by my window stands,
  And every morn they praised God with a hymn,
And, when a certain season passed away,
Five light-green eggs within the building lay.

Above the rush and clatter of the street,
  Devotedly was guarded each green trust,
And the round house was an abode most sweet,
  Roofed with awaiting wings. Better to rust

With iron patience than forego a hope,
And pent life in the shells was felt to grope.

But one dread day, before the sun went down,
A cloud arose, a black and monstrous hand,
That robbed the sunset of its golden crown.
A windy shudder shook the frightened land.
The portals of the storm were opened wide,
And pealing thunder rolled on every side.

Then was it some unchained malicious gust
Troubled the spray whereon the nest was made,
And to the ground the soft-floored dwelling thrust,
And wrecked its hapless store. The birds, dismayed,
Shrilled their unusual grief, and beat the air
With wings whose very whir was like despair.

At dawn, my neighbors, living o'er the way,
  Sent me the whisper that their babe was
      dead;
And, when they led me where the body lay—
  The free, winged spirit's shell, untimely shed—
And the wild cries of their distress I heard,
I thought with pity of each parent bird.

Yet grief is but a cloud that soon is past;
  For there the mated robins came once more,
And built again a nest, compact, and fast
  Upon the tree that grows before my door;
And in it, from the window, could be seen
Five sources of sweet music, new and clean.

Time passed, and to the good home opposite
  Another babe was born, and all the love

That was bereft that fierce and stormy night,
  Fell to the latter child as from above;
And in the nest five yellow mouths one day,
Of their impatient hunger made display.

We love our dead, and hold their memories dear;
  But living love is sweeter than regret.
God's ways are just, and, though they seem severe,
  He can give back with blessings greater yet
Than we have lost. He chastens for some good,
That in our weakness is not understood.

IN THE VALLEY.

THIS is the place—a grove of sighing pines;
Their fallen tassels thatch the roofs with brown,
The long and narrow roofs, 'neath whose confines
No dweller wakens. Though the rains weep down,
Though winds, the mighty mourners, o'er the spot
Go unconsoled, the inmates waken not.

Along the unbusy street my way I keep,
Between the houses tenanted by death,
And seek the place where lies my friend asleep,
Alien to this the life of light and breath.

And here his grave, o'ergrown with heliotrope,
Makes recollection seem as sweet as hope.

For he, my friend, was gentle, wise, and true;
  Pleasant to him a beggar's thankful word;
He spoke no ill of others, and he knew
  And loved clear brooks, green dells, and flower,
    and bird;
And now the flowers strive to return his love
By growing here his humble grave above.

Tears have no courage wherewith they may cease,
  And God by grief is oft misunderstood.
In tears I made complaint of his decease
  Whom I had loved, for he was young and good;
I made complaint that He who rules on high
Should suffer here the young and good to die.

O Death! the warder at the gates of time,
  For evermore to those thy hinge swing wide
Whose hope is flown, whose souls are stained with crime—
  Give way to all who are dissatisfied
With their recurrent days, and long to cease;
Swing wide for such, and to the old give peace.

But close and bar thy dolorous, black gates
  Against the good, the beautiful, the young,
Whose lamp of hope their life illuminates,
  Whose harp-like souls for highest strains are strung.
O warder Death! give way, swing wide for sin;
But close, and bar, and keep the good within.

WHILE THE DAYS GO BY.

I SHALL not say, our life is all in vain,
For peace may cheer at last the barren hearth;
But well I know that, on this weary earth,
Round each joy-island is a sea of pain—
And the days go by.

We watch our hopes, far flickering in the night,
Once radiant torches, lighted in our youth,
To guide, through years, to some broad morn of truth;
But these go out and leave us with no light—
And the days go by.

We see cloud Alps and Andes go and come,
  Dew-thirsty daisies praying them to give:
  We cry, "O Nature, tell us why we live!"
She smiles with beauty, but her lips are dumb—
    And the days go by.

Yet what are we? We breathe, we love, we cease:
  Too soon our little orbits change and fall:
  We are Fate's children, very tired; and all
Are homeless strangers, craving rest and peace—
    And the days go by.

I only ask to drink experience deep:
  And, in the sad, sweet goblet of my years,
  To find love poured with all its smiles and tears;
And quaffing this, I too shall sweetly sleep—
    While the days go by.

WINTER DAYS.

THE winter bourgeons from the north,
The forests bare their sturdy breasts
To every wind that wanders forth,
And in their arms, the lonely nests
That warmed the birdlings long ago,
Are egged with drifted flakes of snow.

No more the robin pipes his lay,
To greet the flushed advance of morn;
He sings in valleys far away;
His heart is with the south to-day;
He cannot shrill among the corn.

For all the hay and corn are down,
  And garnered in the generous barns;
And all the leaves are changed to brown,
  An icy hand is on the tarns;
And on the stream that cuts the plain,
  A diamond necklace, frost and snow,
  Fairer than that which, long ago,
Sir Rohan staked a name to gain.

But colder far than winter days,
  And colder far than snow or frost,
  The heart whose early hope is lost,
Whose birds of joy have ceased to sing;
Dead winter glooms about its ways,
But never promise of the spring.

LOW TIDE.

UNDER the cliff I walk in silence,
While the intrepid waters flow,
And the white birds, lit by the sun into silver,
Glitter against the blue below;
And the tide is low.

Here years ago, in golden weather,
Under the cliff, and close to the sea,
A pledge was given that made me master
Of all that ever was dear to me;
And the tide was low.

Only a little year fled by after,
  Then my bride and I came once more,
And saw the sea, like a bird imprisoned
  Beating its wings 'gainst its bars, the shore;
            And the tide was low.

Now I walk alone by the filmy breakers—
  A voice is hushed I can never forget;
Upon my sea dead calm has fallen,
  My ships are harbored, my sun is set;
            And the tide is low.

AUTUMN BALLAD.

THE orchard-bars are down, my love, and all
across the lawn
The dahlias raise their veinless hands to plead for
summer gone;
And the buckwheat and the barley are so bonny
and so blithe,
That they laugh, with quaint obeisance, at the
reaper with his scythe.

Oh, come out in the orchard, sweet, beneath the
apple-trees,
The happy, golden apples of our own Hesperides;

And pluck the dangling, clustered grapes, in passing 'neath the vine,
Though they weep with luscious tears, my love, and blush to find them wine.

And this babe-cheeked pear, my darling, which I hold up to your mouth,
Seems a hanging nest of sweetness, wrought by summer, winging south;
But the purses of the chestnuts, by the chilly-fingered frost,
Have been opened for his bounty, and their little hoards are lost.

Last night you heard the tempest, love—the wind-entangled pines,
And saw the world-sized clouds that lowered in gloomy, pencilled lines.

I dreamed the storm a sailor's bride who sat beside the sea,
And ever wept like rain, and moaned for that which could not be.

But the morn is rich with sunshine, though the storm may bode the snow;
All the woods in northern distance with their gold and crimson glow.
I have come to seek you, darling, 'mong the queenly dahlias here,
That you may be my dahlia, in this autumn of my year.

DONALD.

O MY white, white, light moon, that saileth in
the sky,
Look down upon the whirling world, for thou art
up so high,
And tell me where my Donald is who sailed across
the sea,
And make a path of silver light to lead him back
to me.

O my white, white, bright moon, thy cheek is
coldly fair,
A little cloud beside thee seems thy wildly float-
ing hair;

And if thou wouldst not have me grow as white
and cold as thee,
Go, make a mighty tide to draw my Donald back
to me.

O my light, white, bright moon, that doth so fond-
ly shine,
There is not a lily in the world but hides its face
from thine;
I too shall go and hide my face close in the dust
from thee,
Unless with light and tide thou bring my Donald
back to me.

LOW LIVES WE LED OF CARE AND SIN.

LOW lives we led of care and sin,
Low lives with but one aim, to win
Our brown and bitter bread.
We dwelt beside a mountain's base,
And ever more its rugged face
Rose sphinx-like overhead.

We could not read a meaning there;
We only saw, high up in air,
A pile of rocks and trees.

We had not climbed the massive height;
Enough for us the small delight
  To sit betimes at ease.

"What good," we asked, "would come, to stand
Upon the wind-swept table-land,
  And look on fields below?"
We sneered, content within the vale;
We had nor will nor wish to scale
  The cliffs where cedars grow.

But haply on a cloudless day
A neighbor on his journey's way,
  Saw, at the sunset hour,
The sun upon our mountain high
Rest like a golden butterfly
  Upon an azure flower.

All thoughts at last perform some use;
The good or ill that they produce
  Must soon or late befall.
When he returned, our neighbor said,
"There may be fertile lands o'erhead
  Upon the mountain-wall."

Straightway we climbed the flinty crags,
And vines above us waved like flags
  Of welcome o'er a town.
Past June-clad plains we wandered by,
And lakes in which the loving sky
  Narcissus-like looked down.

The even grass beneath our feet
Was somewhat greener and more sweet
  Than that which grew below.

We breathed a purer, better air;
Our lives seemed wider and more fair,
  And earth with love aglow.

O ye, long used to care and sin,
Look up! take heart! and strive to win
  A nobler, higher ground!
Think not that Virtue sits alone,
Withdrawn, on frowning peaks of stone,
  Where only thorns abound.

She rather has but quiet dells
Where, with her kin, in peace she dwells,
  And round her all is fair;
While ever, in her pleasant meads,
The flowers of noble thoughts and deeds
  Enrich the healthful air.

A MORNING PASTORAL.

IF someway Bichat's theory be true,
That animal and all organic life
In man combine and culminate—the brain
The animal, the heart organic life—
I know wherefore my love unasked goes out
To meadows, trees, clear brooks, and distant hills,
For thus I am their fellow and their kin.

I chiefly love, while yet the day is new,
To walk among the fields along the road,
And brim my heart with Nature as I pass.
The droning grasshoppers are not in tune;

But here upon a leaf, one seems to drowse,
A sleepy sailor in an open boat,
Rocked on the uneasy billows of the air—
A Palinurus, who, while piloting
The Trojan galleys on disastrous seas,
Drowsed into death, among the Siren rocks.
Here, where I pass, a noisy brook gets force,
And, plunging under alders, leaps along
Down to the fallow, rioting like a boy.
Anon I start a thrush, and up he wings,
And with a trail of music darts away,
Seeking his green republic of high woods,
Where he is citizen, but where his kind
Use melody for speech, and have no flag
Save the thin leaf that shades the hollow nest.
Over the yonder tree-tops flies a crow
That boldly vents his unpopular caw,

And breasts the stubborn wind to gain the shore,
And cram his hungry crop with loathsomeness.
The flowers beside the way are friends of mine,
And once I knew a meditative rose
That never raised its head from bowing down;
But drew its inspiration from the stars.
It bloomed and faded here upon the road,
And, being a poet, wrote upon the air
With fragrance all the beauty of its soul.
I pause beneath an overhanging elm,
Where, cut in granite of the vine-grown wall,
The wide mouth of a quaint, conspicuous face,
Speaks to all thirst with visible eloquence.
Beside it sits a beggar on its trough,
Who craves with quivering lip an alms from me.
I give him from my earning, and go back
Toward the city with a lighter heart.

MAY IN A VILLAGE.

OUR old colonial town is new with May.
The aged elms that clasp across the streets,
Grow greener sleeved with opening buds each day.
Still this year's May the last year's May repeats.
Even the old stone houses half renew
Their youth and beauty as the old trees do.

High over all, like some divine desire
Above our lower thoughts of daily care,
The leaden-colored, tall, religious spire
Adds to the quiet of the spring-time air;

And o'er the roofs the birds create a sea,
That has no shore, of their May melody.

Down through the lowlands now of lightest green,
  The undecided creek winds on its way.
There the lithe willow bends with graceful mien,
  And views its likeness in the depths all day;
While in the orchards, warm with May's warm
    light,
The bride-like fruit-trees dwell, attired in white.

Beyond, the caravan of mountains stands,
  The camel-backs blue-laden with the sky;
And on them oft is laid by unseen hands,
  Like costly merchandise that men may buy,
The silk of sunset clouds, and all the rare
And delicate, wide lace of hazy air.

So, like a caravan, our outlived years
  Loom on the introspective landscape seen
Within the heart. And now when May appears,
  And earth renews its vernal bloom and green,
We but renew our longing, and we say:
"Oh, would life evermore might be all May!

"Would that the bloom of youth that is so brief,
  The bloom, the May, the fulness ripe and fair
Of cheek and limb, might fade not as the leaf—
  Would that the heart might not grow old with care,
Nor love turn bitter, nor fond hope decay;
But soul and body lead a life of May!"

THE STATUE.

IN Athens, when all learning centred there,
  Men reared a column of surpassing height
In honor of Minerva, wise and fair,
  And on the top that dwindled to the sight
A statue of the goddess was to stand,
That wisdom might obtain in all the land.

And he who, with the beauty in his heart
  Seeking in faultless work immortal youth,
Would mould this statue with the finest art,
  Making the wintry marble glow with truth,

Should gain the prize. Two sculptors sought the
fame—
The prize they craved was an enduring name.

Alcamenes soon carved his little best;
But Phidias, beneath a dazzling thought
That like a bright sun in a cloudless west
Lit up his wide, great soul, with pure love
wrought
A statue, and its face of changeless stone
With calm, far-sighted wisdom towered and shone.

Then to be judged the labors were unveiled;
But, at the marble thought, that by degrees
Of hardship Phidias cut, the people railed.
"The lines are coarse; the form too large," said
these;

"And he who sends this rough result of haste
Sends scorn, and offers insult to our taste."

Alcamenes' praised work was lifted high
  Upon the capital where it might stand;
But there it seemed too small, and 'gainst the sky
  Had no proportion from the uplooking land;
So it was lowered and quickly put aside,
And the scorned thought was mounted to be tried.

Surprise swept o'er the faces of the crowd,
  And changed them as a sudden breeze may
      change
A field of fickle grass, and long and loud
  Their mingled shouts to see a sight so strange.
The statue stood completed in its place,
Each coarse line melted to a line of grace.

So bold, great actions that are seen too near,
  Look rash and foolish to unthinking eyes;
They need the past for distance to appear
  In their true grandeur. Let us yet be wise,
And not too soon our neighbor's deed malign,
For what seems coarse is often good and fine.

IN HANGING GARDENS.

IN an old city, so the Rabbins tell,
  Lived a fair lady having youth and wealth,
Who in the hanging gardens loved to dwell;
  And like a shadow, and as still as stealth,
She walked the soundless paths that climbed to kiss
The sun above the grand metropolis.

Here stair on stair, with heavy balustrade,
  And columned hybrids cut in rigid stone,
And vase, and sphinx, and obelisk, arrayed,
  And arched wide bridges over wheelways thrown.

Valleys of heaven the gardens seemed to be,
Or isles of cloud-land in a sunset sea.

The lady, daughter of some prince or king,
  Was loved by one of poor and lowly birth.
He gave her gems enclosed in toy or ring,
  Trifles of cost, of value for their dearth;
But she was used to greater gifts than these,
And their small beauty failed her heart to please.

The Soul is child of Heaven, and when the World,
  Her lover, brings his presents, wealth and fame—
Wealth, a bird jewelled; fame, a ring impearled—
  She is not satisfied. She bears no blame;
But dreams of hanging gardens pathed with bliss
Above a golden-domed metropolis.

FACIEBAT.

AS thoughts possess the fashion of the mood
That gave them birth, so every deed we do,
Partakes of our inborn disquietude
That spurns the old and reaches toward the new.
The noblest works of human art and pride
Show that their makers were not satisfied.

For, looking down the ladder of our deeds,
The rounds seem slender. All past work appears

Unto the doer faulty. The heart bleeds,
  And pale Regret turns weltering in tears,
To think how poor our best has been, how vain,
Beside the excellence we would attain.

THE END.